Straight Forward with Science

ELECTRICITY

Peter Riley

FRANKLIN WATTS
LONDON•SYDNEY

To my granddaughter, Tabitha Grace.

First published in Great Britain in 2015 by The Watts Publishing Group

Copyright text © Peter Riley
(Some content has already appeared in *Straightforward Science: Electricity* (2003)
but has been comprehensively rewritten and redesigned, with additional content, in line with
the National Curriculum for science)

Editor: Julia Bird
Designer: Mo Choy Design

HB ISBN 978 1 4451 3559 5
Library ebook ISBN 978 1 4451 3560 1
Dewey classification number: 537

Photo acknowledgments: Leonid Andronov/Shutterstock: 19b. Badboo/Dreamstime: 17b. p bombaert/
Shutterstock: 22b. Yuriy Boyko/Shutterstock: 13tr. Martyn F Chillmaid/SPL: 17t. Brett Critchley/
Dreamstime: 12bl. danmiz/Shutterstock: 28t, 31. Mark Doherty/Shutterstock: 29r. dolomite summits/
Shutterstock: 20b. Elenarts/Shutterstock: 28bl. grossishut/Shutterstock: 11t. Jiang Hongyan/Shutterstock:
18c. WichaiWongJongJaihan/Shutterstock: 12br. Jamroen Jaiman/Shutterstock: 5tl. Sebastian Kaulitzki/
Shutterstock: 29bl. sabri deniz kizil/Shutterstock: 28br. Gaby Kooljman/Shutterstock: 7t. Thomas Lenne/
Shutterstock: 13tl. manaemedia/Shutterstock: 13b. Marbury/Shutterstock: 14b. Neil Mitchell/Shutterstock:
21t. Cordelia Molloy/SPL: 9r. O6photo/Shutterstock: 13c. Scott David Patterson/Shutterstock: 15b. Sean
Pavone/Shutterstock: front cover, 1. Phovoir/Alamy: 25b. Rtimages/Shutterstock: 9bl. Elena Schweizer/
Shutterstock: 2. Ilya Shcherbaker/Shutterstock: 22t. snapgalleria/Shutterstock: 26c. SnapshotPhotos/
Shutterstock: 2, 5b. Roman Stola/Shutterstock: 9cl. Hein Teh/Dreamstime: 7b. Wiktor Wojtas/Dreamstime: 4t.
Zts/Dreamstime: 12t.

Every attempt has been made to clear copyright. Should there be any inadvertent omission
please apply to the publisher for rectification.

Printed in China

Franklin Watts
An imprint of
Hachette Children's Group
Part of The Watts Publishing Group
Carmelite House
50 Victoria Embankment1
London EC4Y 0DZ

An Hachette UK Company
www.hachette.co.uk
www.franklinwatts.co.uk

FSC
www.fsc.org
MIX
Paper from
responsible sources
FSC® C104740

Contents

Electricity around us

Electricity plays a very important part in our lives. It powers an alarm clock to wake us up in the morning. It provides heat and light in our homes and powers television sets and computers. Some cars can even run on electricity.

I Electricity is being used to charge the battery of this car so it can power the car's engine when it is driven away.

A SIMPLE CIRCUIT

Electricity is a form of energy, like heat and light. It moves along wires from an electrical supply to the object it is powering. The movement of electricity is called the flow, or the current. In order for a current to flow, electricity has to move along a circular path called a circuit.

A simple circuit can be made from a cell, some wire, a switch and a bulb. A cell is what we call a battery in everyday life. A battery is really a group of cells.

The bulb lights up when the switch is closed. This shows that electricity is moving around the circuit.

The battery is the store of electrical energy.

The wires let the electricity flow through them.

The switch can be closed to make the circuit complete, or opened to break it.

CIRCUITS EVERYWHERE

There are circuits in every piece of electrical equipment we use. A torch has a circuit with two cells, a light bulb and a switch connected by metal strips.

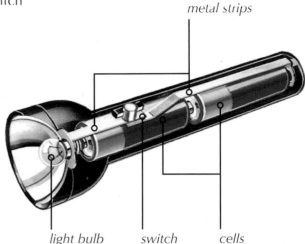

metal strips

light bulb   *switch*   *cells*

CLOSING THE GAPS

Wires are joined to terminals (see page 6) on the battery or cell. The places where the wires connect to the switch and the bulb are called the contacts. Electricity will only flow around the circuit if the wires are connected to the terminals and contacts and the switch is on. A gap anywhere in the circuit breaks it and stops the flow of electricity.

INVESTIGATE

Take the cells out of a torch and look for the other parts of the circuit. Press the switch and see how it makes and breaks the circuit.

❚ These buildings have circuits on every floor. When they are switched on, electricity lights the rooms and powers any electrical equipment.

Cells and batteries

In a simple circuit, the current of electricity is made in a cell or a battery. The electricity made when the simple circuit is switched on is much weaker than mains electricity. It can be used for making simple scientific enquiries about electricity.

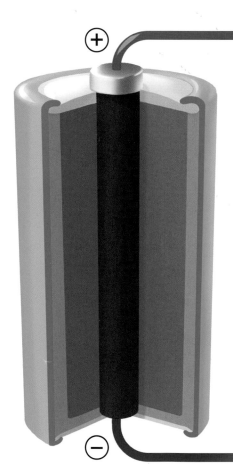

A CELL

A cell has a metal case and contains a paste. In the paste are chemicals. They produce the current of electricity that flows around a circuit when the circuit is switched on.

The two places where wires are attached to the cell are called the terminals. One terminal is marked with a + sign. It is called the positive terminal. The other terminal is marked with a – sign. It is called the negative terminal. The current of electricity always flows around the circuit from the negative terminal to the positive terminal.

A BATTERY

A battery is a group of cells joined together. The positive terminal of one cell is joined to the negative terminal of the cell next to it. The cells are placed next to each other in a box. The positive and negative terminals of the battery stick out of the top of the box.

In this lemon clock, each lemon acts as a cell. The metal sticking into the lemons and the lemon juice inside the fruits make a current of electricity. This flows round the circuit and makes the clock work.

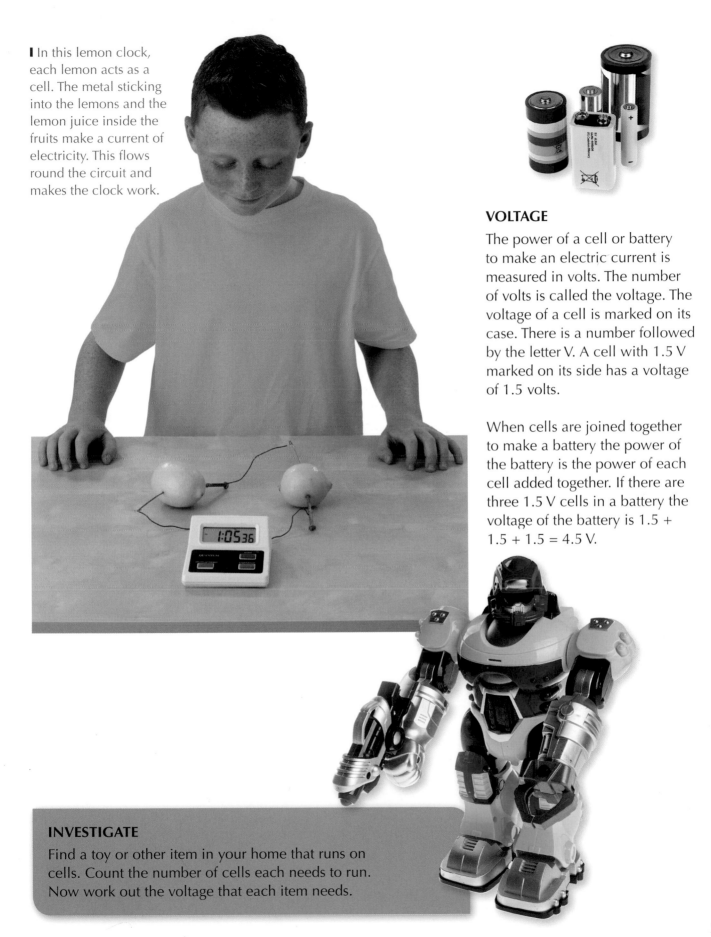

VOLTAGE

The power of a cell or battery to make an electric current is measured in volts. The number of volts is called the voltage. The voltage of a cell is marked on its case. There is a number followed by the letter V. A cell with 1.5 V marked on its side has a voltage of 1.5 volts.

When cells are joined together to make a battery the power of the battery is the power of each cell added together. If there are three 1.5 V cells in a battery the voltage of the battery is $1.5 + 1.5 + 1.5 = 4.5$ V.

INVESTIGATE

Find a toy or other item in your home that runs on cells. Count the number of cells each needs to run. Now work out the voltage that each item needs.

Conductors and insulators

Electricity travels around a circuit because the wire in a circuit allows electricity to flow through it. The wire is a conductor of electricity. Electricity does not pass through all materials. Materials that do not conduct electricity are called electrical insulators.

TESTING MATERIALS

A simple way to sort materials into conductors and insulators is to set up a circuit with a gap in it. The material to be tested is placed across the gap. If the material is a conductor, electricity flows around the circuit and makes the bulb light up. If the material is an insulator, electricity does not flow and the bulb does not light up.

CONDUCTORS

Any metal material tested in the circuit will make the bulb light up because all metals are conductors. One substance that is not a metal but conducts electricity is graphite. Graphite is the black substance that is used to make the lead in a pencil, among other things. Water is also a good conductor of electricity.

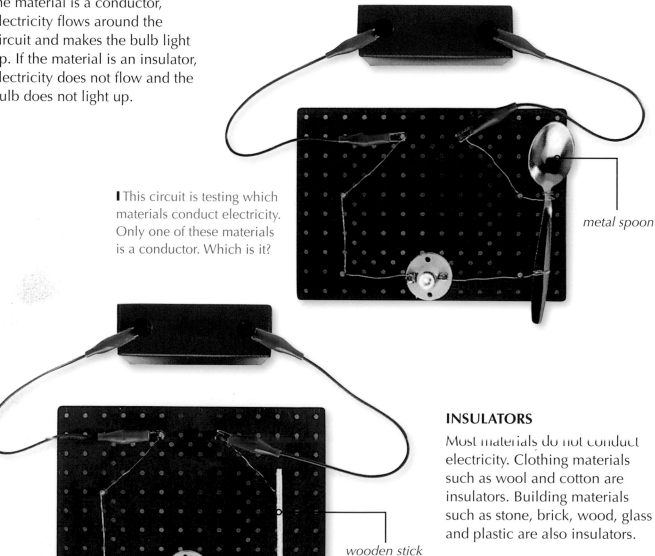

▌This circuit is testing which materials conduct electricity. Only one of these materials is a conductor. Which is it?

metal spoon

wooden stick

INSULATORS

Most materials do not conduct electricity. Clothing materials such as wool and cotton are insulators. Building materials such as stone, brick, wood, glass and plastic are also insulators.

❙ These pottery discs are insulators and are used to hold power cables safely on electricity pylons.

pottery discs ────────

KEEPING SAFE

Electricity is dangerous and should never be touched. Care must be taken when handling any electrical equipment. You can keep safe by only touching the plastic parts of an electrical object and by drying your hands before touching light switches.

❙ An electricity sign warns you to stay away from high levels of electricity.

❙ Electricity is conducted to equipment through a metal lead and plug. The lead and plug are covered in plastic to stop the electricity from reaching your hand.

INVESTIGATE

Set up the circuit shown on page 8. Test some metal, graphite, wood and plastic to see which ones light up the light bulb.

Switches

The flow of electricity in a circuit is controlled by a switch. It either lets electricity flow around the circuit or it stops it from flowing.

ON...

A switch is a piece of metal that can be moved. One end of the metal is connected to a wire in the circuit. The other end can be moved to touch a contact in the circuit. When the end is touching the contact the switch is 'on'. The 'on' switch is also said to be closed because it has closed the gap in the circuit. The 'on' or closed switch lets electricity pass through the circuit.

...AND OFF

The switch is 'off' or open when the end of the metal is not touching the contact. A gap is made in the circuit. Electricity cannot pass through the gap, so electricity cannot pass around the circuit.

THE LIGHT SWITCH ON THE WALL

Inside the light switch on the wall are two pieces of metal. When you press the switch, a piece of plastic pushes on one of the pieces of metal and moves it. When the light is switched on, the metal is moved to touch the other piece of metal. The electricity can now flow through the circuit and the light comes on.

When the light is switched off, the metal in the switch is moved away from the other piece of metal. The electricity stops flowing and the light goes out.

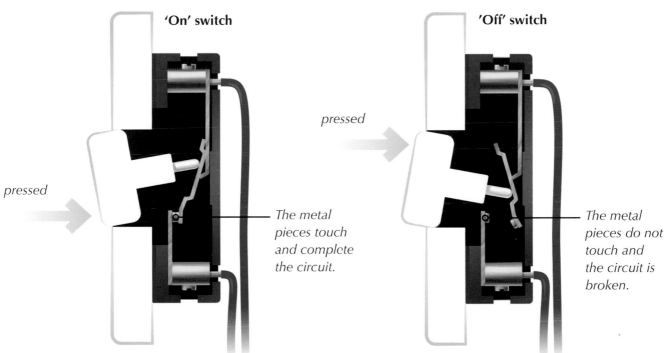

'On' switch

'Off' switch

pressed

pressed

The metal pieces touch and complete the circuit.

The metal pieces do not touch and the circuit is broken.

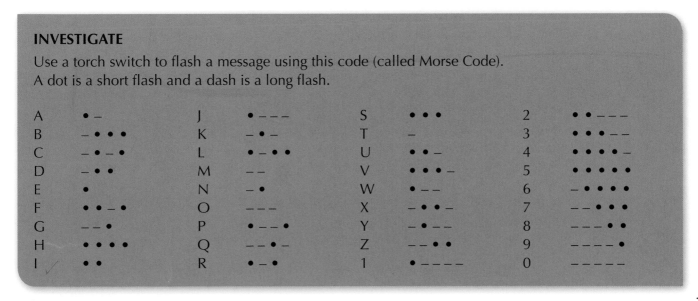

INVESTIGATE

Use a torch switch to flash a message using this code (called Morse Code).
A dot is a short flash and a dash is a long flash.

A	• –	J	• – – –	S	• • •	2	• • – – –
B	– • • •	K	– • –	T	–	3	• • • – –
C	– • – •	L	• – • •	U	• • –	4	• • • • –
D	– • •	M	– –	V	• • • –	5	• • • • •
E	•	N	– •	W	• – –	6	– • • • •
F	• • – •	O	– – –	X	– • • –	7	– – • • •
G	– – •	P	• – – •	Y	– • – –	8	– – – • •
H	• • • •	Q	– – • –	Z	– – • •	9	– – – – •
I	• •	R	• – •	1	• – – – –	0	– – – – –

ICM1405>5595

Heat and light

The metal in a wire pushes against the flow of electricity passing though it. This push is called resistance. The current of electricity has to push harder than the resistance to get through the wire. If the resistance is very strong (or 'high') the electricity may make the wire hot as it pushes through it.

HOT WIRES

A kettle has a high-resistance wire contained in a waterproof metal tube. When the kettle is switched on the wire gets hot and boils the water. A toaster also has high-resistance wires. When it is switched on the wires glow, give out heat and toast bread.

I The resistance wire in a kettle is contained in a metal tube. The wire and tube do not touch. This stops the electricity reaching the water.

FUSES

A fuse contains a wire which melts if the electric current gets too high. When this happens we say the fuse has 'blown'. The melted wire stops the flow of electricity and prevents the high current causing a fire.

I The heat from these wires has toasted the bread.

I Fuses are used in many circuits to protect electrical equipment.

I Filament light bulbs can be used in investigations on electricity in schools.

I Low energy bulbs help to conserve the fuels used in power stations, including precious fossil fuels.

LIGHT

A filament light bulb has a high-resistance coil of wire in it. This is called the filament. Its resistance is so high that when electricity passes through it the wire gets so hot it glows and gives out light.

LOW ENERGY LIGHT BULBS

These bulbs use about a fifth of the electrical energy of a filament light bulb. They do not rely on a high-resistance wire coil. Instead, each one is a glass tube filled with mercury vapour and coated on the inside with a chemical containing phosphorus. When electricity passes through the lamp, the mercury gives out ultraviolet light which makes the coating shine and give out light.

I Fluorescent lights are long tubes sometimes called strip lights. They work in the same way as low energy lamps.

LIGHT EMITTING DIODE (LED)

An LED contains a material called a semiconductor. It is enclosed in a plastic cap. When electricity passes through the semiconductor it gives out light. LEDs also use much less energy than filament light bulbs. They are used as standby lights on electrical appliances such as televisions, and in the illuminated display on alarm clocks, traffic lights and smartphones.

I LEDs are used to light the liquid crystal displays (LCDs) used on many electronic devices.

INVESTIGATE

How many light sources are used around your home? Are they filament bulbs, low energy lamps, fluorescent lights or LEDs?

Controlling the flow

S ometimes we want to add more than one light bulb to a circuit. There are two ways in which they can be joined up: in series or in parallel.

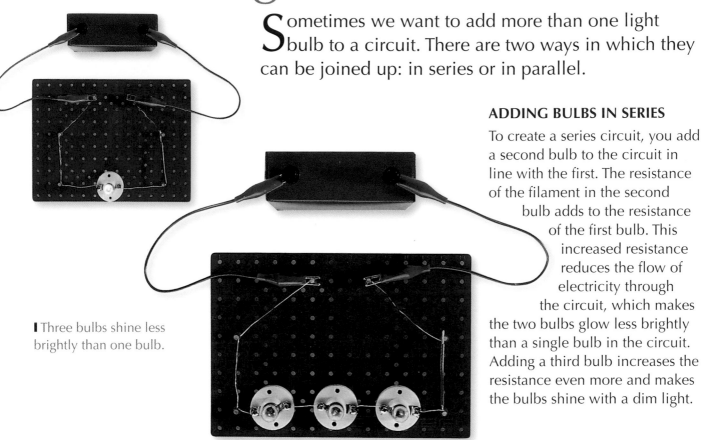

ADDING BULBS IN SERIES

To create a series circuit, you add a second bulb to the circuit in line with the first. The resistance of the filament in the second bulb adds to the resistance of the first bulb. This increased resistance reduces the flow of electricity through the circuit, which makes the two bulbs glow less brightly than a single bulb in the circuit. Adding a third bulb increases the resistance even more and makes the bulbs shine with a dim light.

❚ Three bulbs shine less brightly than one bulb.

❚ Fairy lights are wired in series. In the past, when the filament in the bulb failed, all the bulbs went out. Today each bulb has a wire which takes over when a filament breaks and conducts electricity so all the other bulbs can stay alight.

ADDING BULBS IN PARALLEL

A bulb can also be added to a circuit in parallel. To do this, a new circuit is created for the new bulb. When the current is switched on it flows through each bulb separately.

The resistance of the filament in the second bulb does not add to the resistance of the filament in the first bulb. More current passes through bulbs in parallel than through bulbs in series.

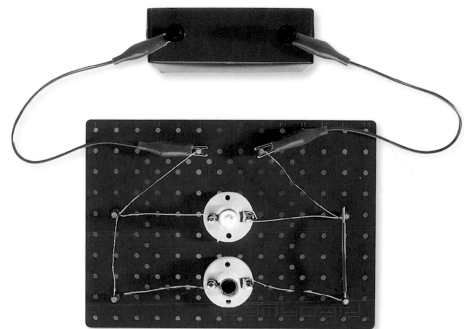

▮ These bulbs are arranged in parallel so that if one is removed the other keeps shining.

INVESTIGATE

Make a circuit with one cell and one bulb, then build up a series circuit with three bulbs and two cells, adding one component at a time. Record what happens after you have added each component.

CELLS IN CIRCUITS

A cell contains the force to push a current of electricity around a circuit. When cells are arranged in series, the voltage in the circuit is increased and each cell provides a pushing force to the current, making bulbs shine more brightly. If cells are arranged in parallel the voltage is not increased and the pushing force is shared out among the cells. This means that bulbs do not shine more brightly but the cells can keep pushing for longer and the bulbs shine for longer.

▮ The bulbs in homes and streets do not go out if one bulb fails. They all stay on. This is due to the way they are connected in parallel with each other.

Electricity and magnetism

In the early 19th century a scientist called Hans Christian Ørsted was experimenting with an electric circuit. One wire was near a compass. When the circuit was switched on, the compass needle moved. The electricity in the wire was affecting the magnetism in the compass. From this observation electromagnets were developed.

MAKING MAGNETS

A piece of a magnetic material such as iron or steel is made up of millions of tiny magnetic regions called domains. In an unmagnetised piece of iron the domains point in all directions and the metal cannot attract other magnetic materials. However, if an electric current is allowed to flow close to an iron nail it makes the domains in the metal line up and turns the nail into a magnet.

▌The domains in an iron bar when the electric current is switched off.

▌The domains in an iron bar when the electric current is switched on.

THE ELECTROMAGNET

This discovery led to the invention of the electromagnet. A simple electromagnet can be made in the following way: a long piece of wire is wound around an iron nail to make a coil. This coil of wire is called a solenoid. Each end of the solenoid is then connected into a circuit. One end is connected to a contact of a switch and the other to a terminal of a battery. The nail becomes a magnet. However, if the current is switched off the domains no longer line up and the nail becomes unmagnetised again. This means that any material that has been attracted to the nail no longer sticks to it and falls away.

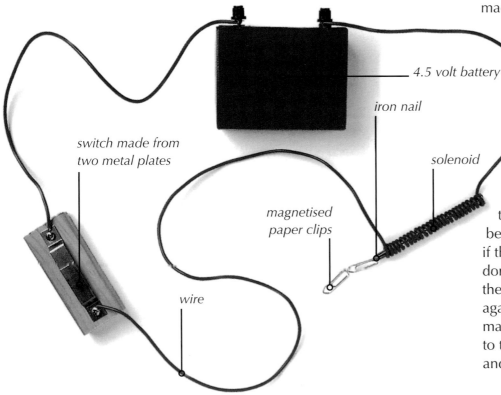

4.5 volt battery

iron nail

switch made from two metal plates

solenoid

magnetised paper clips

wire

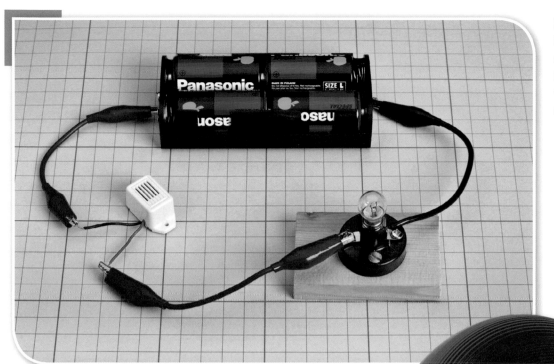

I The electromagnet in a buzzer switches on and off rapidly to make the buzzer vibrate and produce a sound.

BUZZERS

A simple buzzer contains an electromagnet. It has to be wired into a circuit in a certain way for the buzzer to work. One wire from the electromagnet is red. This must be connected to the positive terminal of the cell or battery. The other wire is black and must be connected to the negative terminal.

MAKING NOISE

When the switch is closed, electricity passes through the solenoid of the electromagnet and it attracts a piece of metal. As soon as it touches the electromagnet it stops the electricity flowing. The electromagnet can no longer attract it and it moves back. As soon as it does this it makes the current flow again and is attracted to the electromagnet again. All this movement takes place many times a second and causes the vibration that we hear as a buzz.

I The electromagnet in this alarm clock switches on and off rapidly to move the hammer between the bells.

INVESTIGATE

Set up a buzzer in a circuit with a switch and cell. Predict what will happen when you add another cell and then try it.

The electric motor

When electricity flows through a coil of wire, it makes the coil behave like a magnet. If a wire coil with a current going through it is put between a pair of magnets, the coil spins. The spinning coil can be used to make an electric motor.

THE POLES OF A MAGNET

Magnets have two places where their magnetic force is strongest. These places are called the north pole and the south pole.

▮ If a north pole and a south pole are brought together and released, their forces pull them together.

▮ If a north pole and a north pole are brought together and released, their forces push each other away.

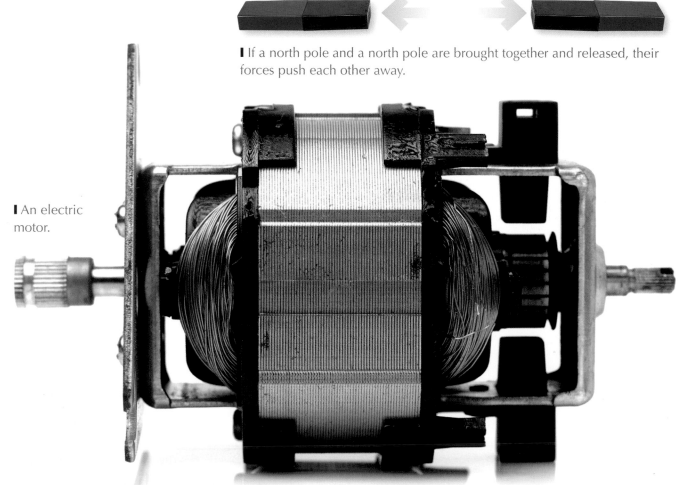

▮ An electric motor.

HOW A MOTOR WORKS

Inside an electric motor there is a coil of wire with a current running through it. The current of electricity gives the coil of wire a north pole and a south pole. The coil is placed between two magnets.

I The magnetic poles on the coil are used to keep the coil spinning.

MAKING IT SPIN

The north pole of the coil is attracted to the south pole of the magnet, and the south pole of the coil is attracted to the north pole of the magnet. These forces of attraction turn the coil around so that the south pole of the magnet faces the north pole of the coil.

CHANGING DIRECTION

The contacts in the coil are set up so that at this point the current changes direction and flows around the coil in the opposite direction. The part of the coil facing the north pole of the magnet now also has a north pole. The coil is repelled by the magnet and spins around again.

ROUND AND ROUND

The current continues to change direction, and this makes the coil spin around and around. If the coil is connected to a wheel through a motor shaft, the wheel spins around as the coil spins.

ELECTRIC MOTORS EVERYWHERE

Small electric motors are used to turn records, CDs and DVDs. Larger electric motors drive washing machines and power drills. A huge electric motor is used to pull a train.

I An electric motor turns the wheels on an electric train.

Generating electricity

As we have seen, if a coil with a current passing through it is put between two magnets, it can be made to spin. In a similar way, if a spinning magnet is put near a wire coil, an electric current will be generated in the coil.

THE DYNAMO

A device called a dynamo is used to generate electricity to light the lamps in some bicycles, among other things. A side wall or bottle dynamo has a wheel at the top. When it is dark and light is needed, the cyclist clicks the wheel into place so that it touches the tyre, turns with it and the dynamo generates electricity to light the lamp. There is a second kind of bicycle dynamo called a hub dynamo which is attached to the centre of a bicycle wheel. It works in the same way as the bottle dynamo.

dynamo wheel *bicycle tyre*

coil *cable which connects the coil to the lamp*

magnet

❚ Electricity provides light for cyclists to see the road in the dark.

THE ELECTRIC GENERATOR

Most of the electricity we use is generated in power stations. An electric generator at a power station is like a gigantic dynamo. Around the generator walls are huge coils of wire and down its centre is a magnet shaped like a cylinder. The magnet is attached to a shaft which passes out of the generator.

CREATING THE CURRENT

In most kinds of power stations, the generator shaft is attached to turbine blades. Using a fuel such as coal or oil, water is heated in a boiler to make steam which is directed over the blades and makes them turn and spin the shaft. The shaft spins the magnet in the generator. The spinning magnet generates a current of electricity in the wires. The current is passed along cables in the air or underground to towns and cities far away.

I This power station burns coal to make steam (see below). The steam condenses in cooling towers but some escapes to form clouds of water droplets in the air.

INVESTIGATE

Find out about the different kinds of power stations. Do they all heat water to make steam in the same way? Do they all use steam to make the turbines spin? Do power stations damage the environment? Present the evidence for your answers.

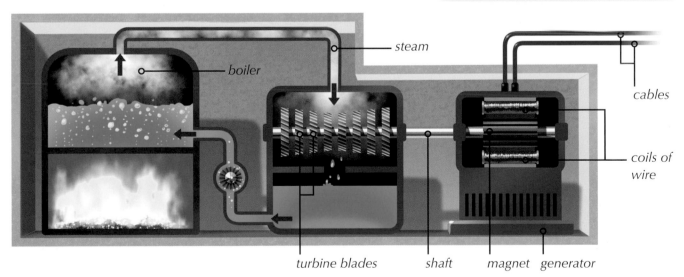

steam

boiler

cables

coils of wire

turbine blades   shaft   magnet   generator

ENERGY SOURCES

Fuels such as coal, gas and oil are non-renewable energy resources. One day they will all be used up. Scientists are working on developing power stations which run on renewable resources such as the wind, waves and solar power.

Electricity in your home

The electricity from a power station travels through a cable to a substation in your neighbourhood. Here its power is reduced a little before travelling through another cable into your home.

MONITORING THE FLOW

Electricity first passes through a meter which records how much electricity is used, then moves into the consumer unit. This contains fuses or devices to break circuits if the current in them gets too strong. Electricity can flow from the consumer unit to any of the circuits in the house that are switched on.

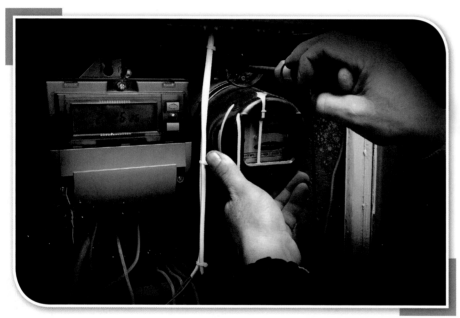

I This meter is being installed to measure the amount of electricity being used in a building.

DIFFERENT CIRCUITS

There is a circuit on each floor of a building which has sockets in the wall. Many kinds of electrical device can be plugged into it. This circuit is called a ring main. There is also a ceiling light circuit on each floor. The circuits are opened and closed by switches on the walls. An electric cooker has its own circuit because it uses a large amount of current.

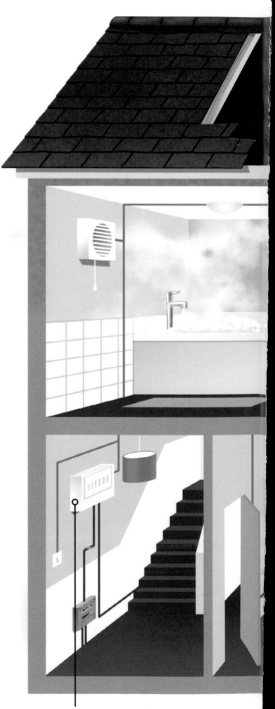

consumer unit

USES OF ELECTRICITY

Electricity in a house provides energy for everything from boiling a kettle to cooking food and heating rooms through electric fires and radiators. Light shines from light bulbs and tubes, and glows from LEDs and liquid-crystal displays as electricity passes through them. Electric motors spin DVDs and turn everything from microwave ovens to washing machines, dryers, food mixers and power drills.

Electricity flows through aerials and satellite dishes to pick up signals that make radios and televisions work. It gives power to a computer and links it to the Internet.

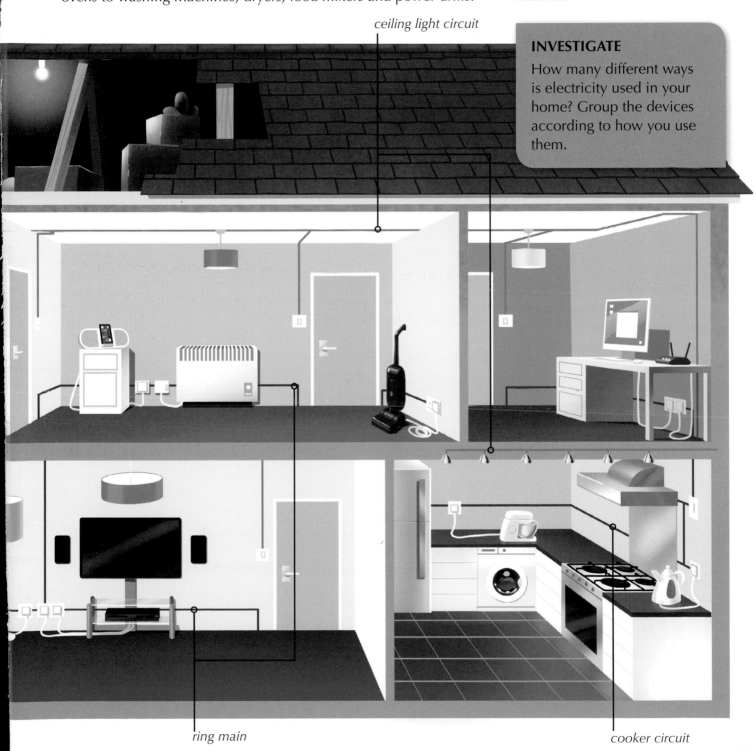

ceiling light circuit

INVESTIGATE

How many different ways is electricity used in your home? Group the devices according to how you use them.

ring main

cooker circuit

Circuit diagrams

When scientists complete any investigation, they record their results. If they study electricity, scientists also record the arrangement of components in an electrical circuit. This helps them to remember the circuit, especially if it is complicated, and also allows other people to assemble the circuit and check the scientists' results.

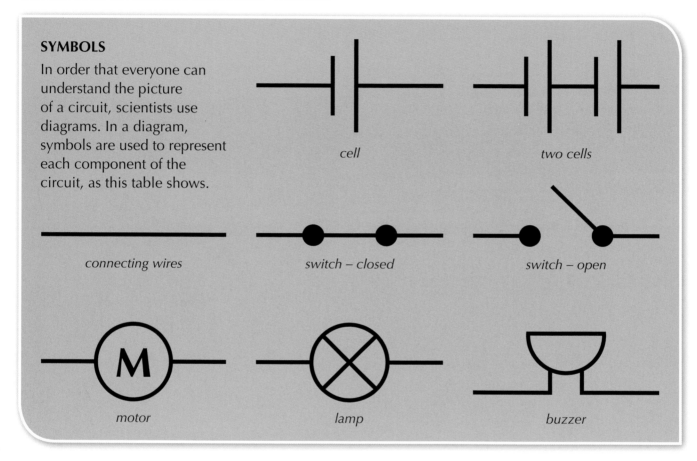

SYMBOLS

In order that everyone can understand the picture of a circuit, scientists use diagrams. In a diagram, symbols are used to represent each component of the circuit, as this table shows.

cell

two cells

connecting wires

switch – closed

switch – open

motor

lamp

buzzer

WIRES

In a circuit, wires are not drawn as they may appear in the circuit with bends or curves. They are always drawn as straight lines. This is the circuit diagram of the components in the picture on page 25.

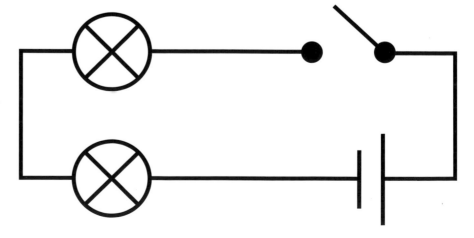

CELLS AND TERMINALS

When cells are arranged in series in a circuit they must be connected in a special way. The positive terminal of one cell must be connected to the negative terminal of the next cell – just as in a battery. This must also be recorded in the circuit diagram. In the symbol for a cell the long vertical line stands for the positive terminal and the short vertical line stands for the negative terminal (see page 24). This must be remembered when drawing in two or more cells in series.

I These components are being assembled into the circuit shown in the diagram on page 24.

USING CIRCUIT DIAGRAMS

Every piece of electrical equipment such as a television or a washing machine has a circuit diagram to show how the components are arranged to make the device work. These are used by people assembling the devices and engineers who repair them.

INVESTIGATE

Draw some circuit diagrams. Each one should feature either a buzzer or a motor or one or more lamps. Make a circuit for each one or challenge a friend to make it.

I These electricians are studying a circuit diagram of a building so that they can wire it correctly.

Static electricity

Every substance is made of tiny particles called atoms. Inside each atom are even smaller particles called electrons. When certain substances are rubbed together, the electrons move from one substance to the other. This gives both substances an electric charge which does not move. This is called static electricity.

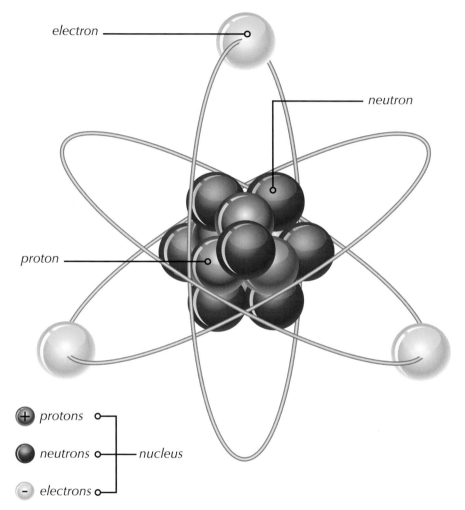

electron

neutron

proton

(+) protons

● neutrons — nucleus

(-) electrons

I Protons and neutrons are part of a substance's nucleus (control centre). Electrons form a 'cloud' around it.

MAKING STATIC ELECTRICITY

There are two kinds of electric charge. They are called positive charge and negative charge. An electron has a negative charge.

If a balloon is rubbed on a woollen jumper, some electrons leave the jumper and collect on the balloon. The extra electrons on the balloon give it a negative electric charge. The lack of electrons on the jumper give it a positive charge.

The two different charges attract each other. When the balloon is pressed onto the jumper, it stays in place because the negative charge on the balloon attracts the positive charge on the jumper. The two charged objects are pulled together, as you can see below.

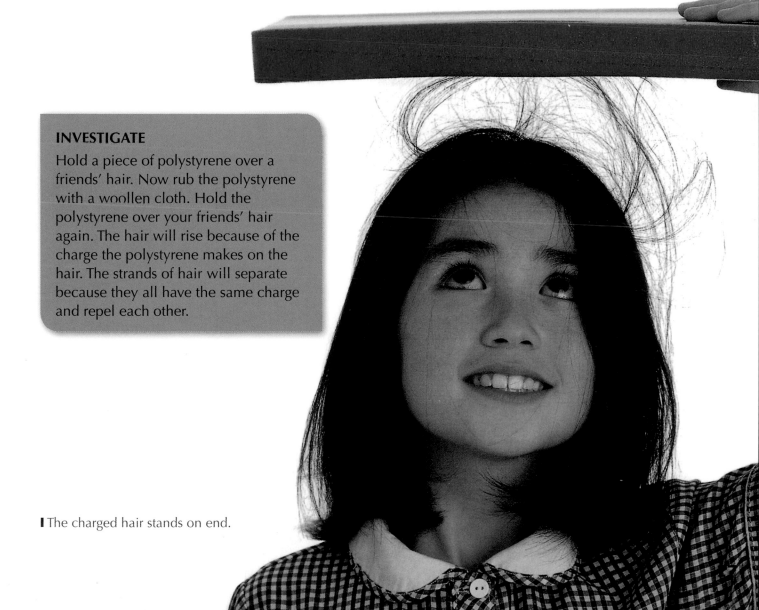

These scraps of paper have leapt up onto the charged pen.

ONE CHARGE MAKING ANOTHER

A charged object can drive away electrons from the surface of another object, or it can draw more electrons to its surface. When this happens the surface of the second object also becomes charged.

A plastic pen becomes negatively charged when it is rubbed with a cloth. If it is placed near a small scrap of paper the negative charge makes one surface of the scrap of paper positive. The strength of attraction between the two charges makes the paper scrap spring up to the pen and stick to it.

INVESTIGATE

Hold a piece of polystyrene over a friends' hair. Now rub the polystyrene with a woollen cloth. Hold the polystyrene over your friends' hair again. The hair will rise because of the charge the polystyrene makes on the hair. The strands of hair will separate because they all have the same charge and repel each other.

The charged hair stands on end.

Electricity in nature

Electricity is not just found in batteries and power stations. It is found throughout nature – from inside storm clouds to the nerves that carry messages around your body.

LIGHTNING

Lightning is a form of electricity you can see. It is made when a very large charge of static electricity builds up in a storm cloud. The static electricity is made by the winds inside the clouds rubbing ice particles together. The top of the cloud becomes positively charged and the bottom of the cloud becomes negatively charged.

I Lightning is most often seen in tropical areas where warm and cold air meet.

TYPES OF LIGHTNING

When the charges get very high, the air between them can no longer act as an insulator and a huge current of electricity flows. This makes a flash of light inside the cloud called sheet lightning.

The negative charge at the base of a storm cloud drives away the negative charge from the surface of the ground and makes it positively charged. The difference in charge between the cloud and the ground may become so high that lightning flashes between them. This is called forked lightning.

When lightning flashes, it destroys all the charges.

28

ELECTRIC FISH

The electric eel of South American rivers, the electric catfish of African rivers and the electric ray, which is found in most seas, all have parts of their bodies which can make electricity. They use this electricity to catch fish by releasing electricity into the water around them. The electricity does not harm the electric fish, but it kills or stuns any fish nearby. The dead or stunned fish are then easy to catch and eat.

❙ The marbled torpedo electric ray can deliver an electric shock of around 70–80 volts.

ELECTRICITY IN THE BODY

The brain and nerves of humans and animals make electric currents which flow through them. The electric currents control the activity of the body and keep it alive.

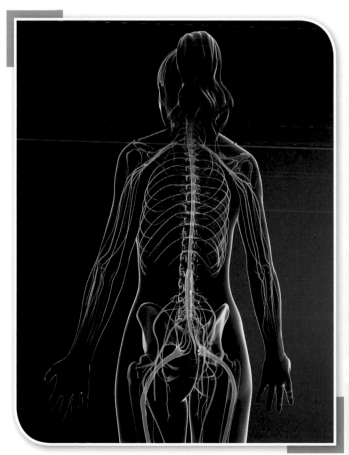

❙ The nervous system sends messages around the human body via electric current.

INVESTIGATE

Find out how fast messages travel from your eye to your hand muscles by asking a friend to drop a ruler between your finger and thumb. How fast can you catch it?

Glossary

atom – a tiny particle which is made of even smaller particles. At its centre is a nucleus made from particles called protons and neutrons. Moving around the nucleus are smaller particles still. They are called electrons.

attract – to pull close.

battery – a groups of cells joined together.

cell – a metal container that holds the chemicals that make the electricity flow in a circuit. In everyday life we call it a battery.

circuit – a path along which a current of electricity can be made to pass. It has a source of electricity such as a cell, wires and a switch.

component – an item that is part of a circuit such as a cell, wire or bulb.

contact – a piece of metal that connects a wire to a device in a circuit.

current – the flow of electricity in a circuit.

domain – group of atoms in iron or steel that can behave like microscopic magnets.

dynamo – a device which contains a magnet and a wire coil.

electrical conductor – a material such as a metal that a current of electricity can pass through.

electrical insulator – a material such as pottery that a current of electricity cannot pass through.

electromagnet – a magnet made with a wire coiled around a piece of iron. It only has magnetic power when a current of electricity flows through the wire.

electron – a very small particle in an atom which has a negative electrical charge. Electrons can be moved between some materials by rubbing the materials together.

element – a wire with a high resistance which produces heat when the circuit is switched on.

filament – a coiled thread of wire in a filament light bulb through which electricity passes. When this happens, the metal in the filament becomes so hot that it gives out light.

fuse – a device which contains a wire that melts and breaks a circuit if the current in it becomes too high.

generator – a machine at a power station which contains a magnet surrounded by coils of wire. The magnet is connected to a rod called a shaft. When the shaft is made to spin, the magnet spins too. The spinning magnet generates electricity in the coils of wire.

graphite – a black substance made from carbon which conducts electricity like a metal. It is used to make the lead in pencils.

lead – a plastic-coated wire for carrying electricity from the mains to an electrical device such as a computer.

liquid crystal display (lcd) – an arrangement of liquid crystals and electrical circuits used in some clocks and calculators to display numbers.

low energy bulb – a bulb which uses much less electricity, and therefore energy, than a filament light bulb.

mains electricity – electricity that is produced in a power station and delivered through underground or overground cables.

Morse code – a code of dots and dashes invented by Samuel Morse in 1837 to send messages by electrical currents on long wires called telegraph wires.

motor shaft – a rod connected to a wire coil in a motor. It is also connected to a wheel that is used to provide movement, such as to turn compact discs and parts of a washing machine.

nerve – a long fibre that carries electrical messages around the body.

non-renewable energy – energy sources such as coal, oil and gas which cannot be replaced.

parallel circuit – a circuit in which some components are arranged side by side.

repel – to push away.

semiconductor – a material which can be made to vary the amount of electricity it conducts.

series circuit – a circuit in which all the components are arranged in a loop.

static electricity – electricity that stays in one place and does not move as a current.

substation – a place where the voltage of electricity from a power station is made weaker before it travels on to homes or businesses.

switch – a device which is used to make the electricity flow around a circuit or to stop it flowing around a circuit.

terminal – the place where a wire is connected to a cell or a battery.

voltage – a measure of the electrical power of a cell or battery.